101 COLORING BOOK VINTAGE CARS & TRUCKS

THIS BOOK BELONGS TO

....

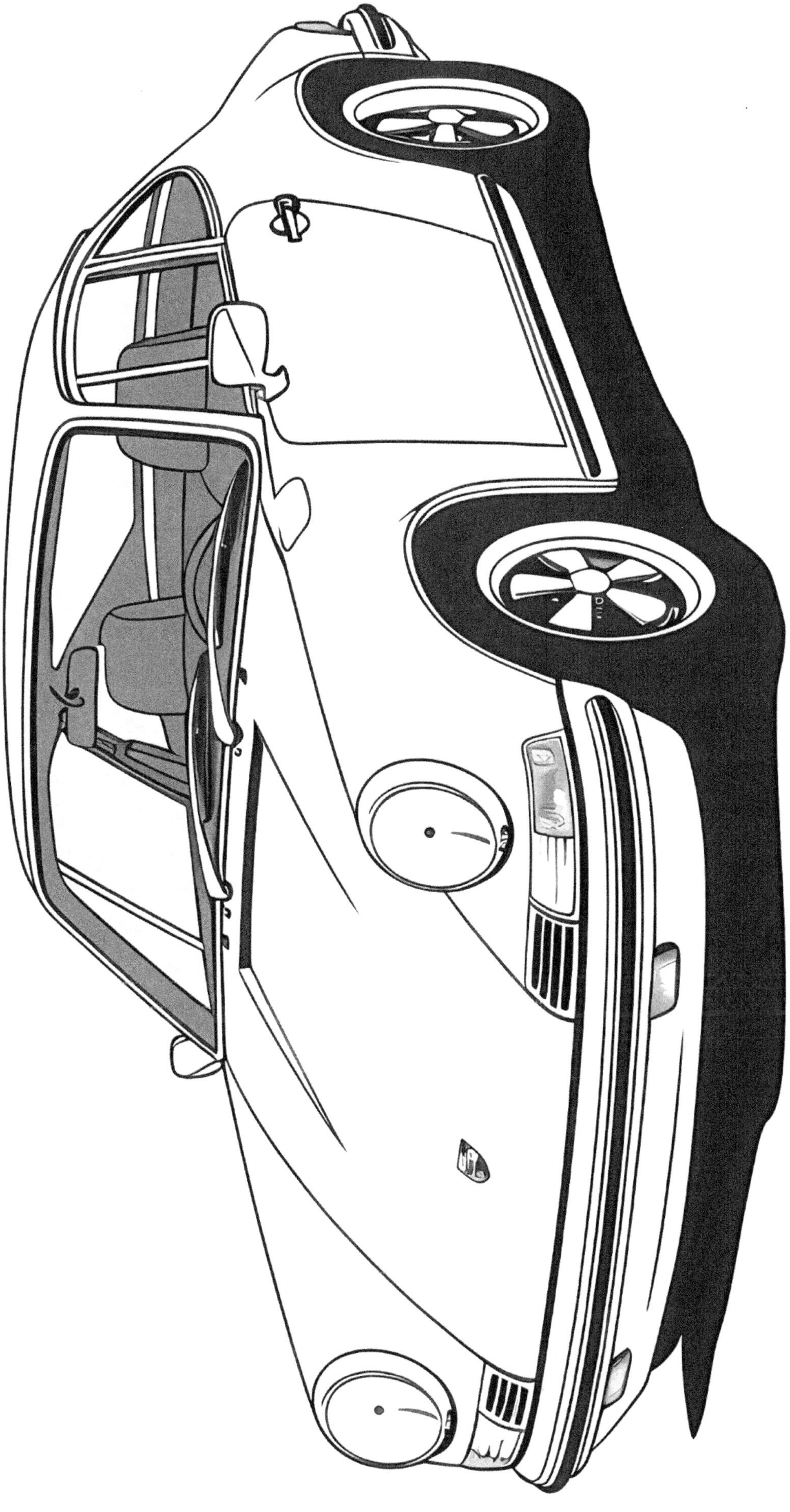

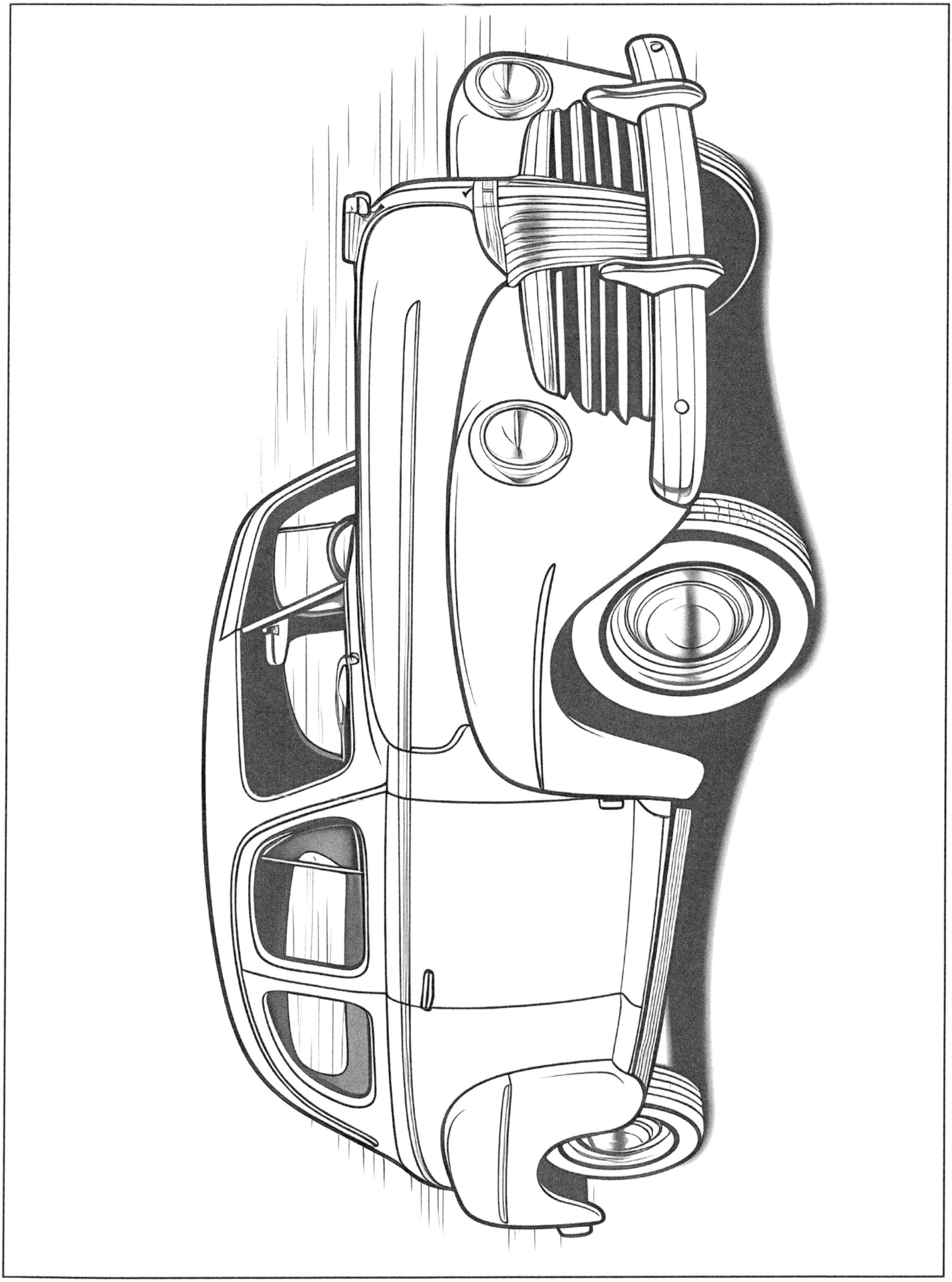

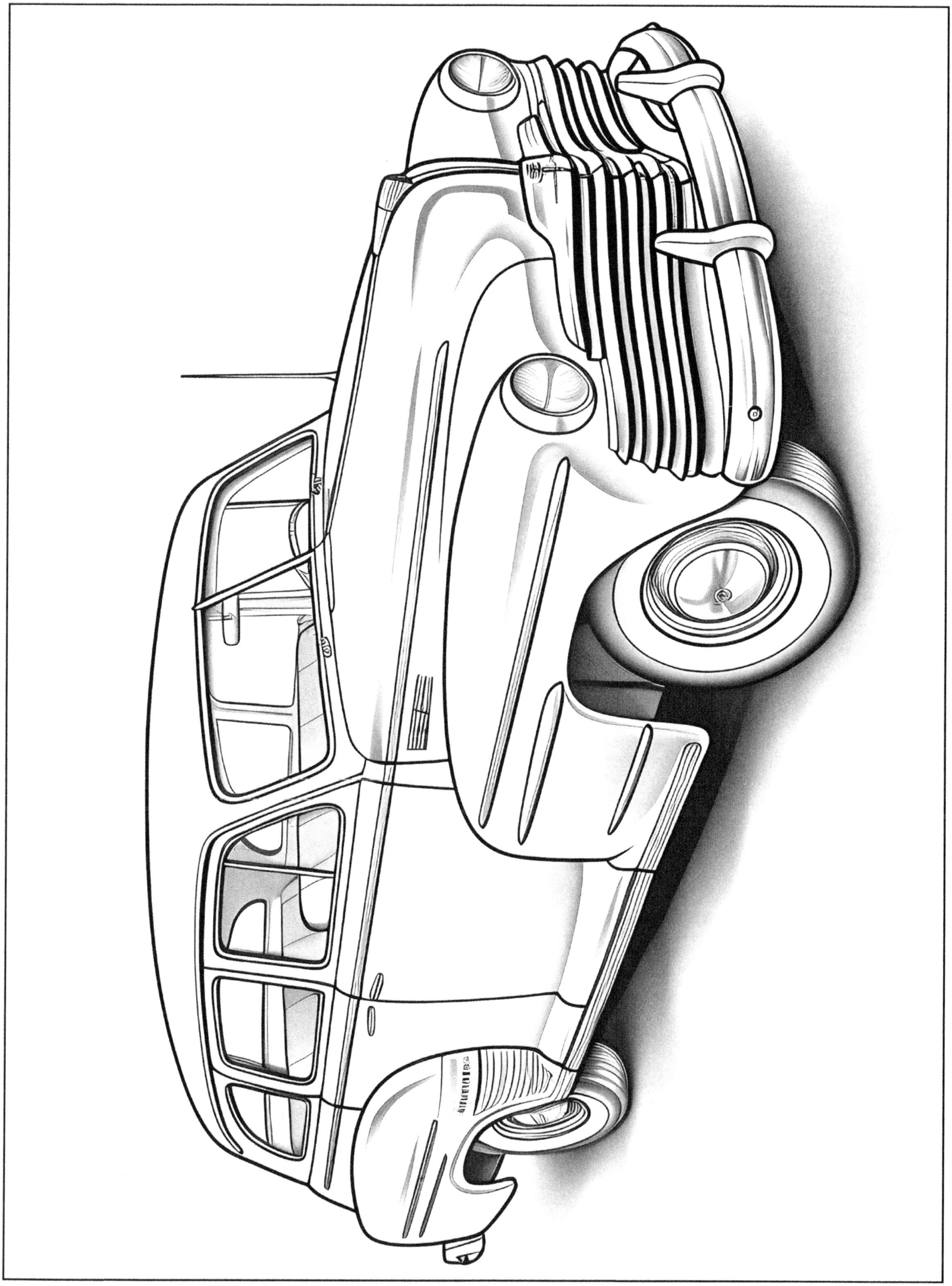

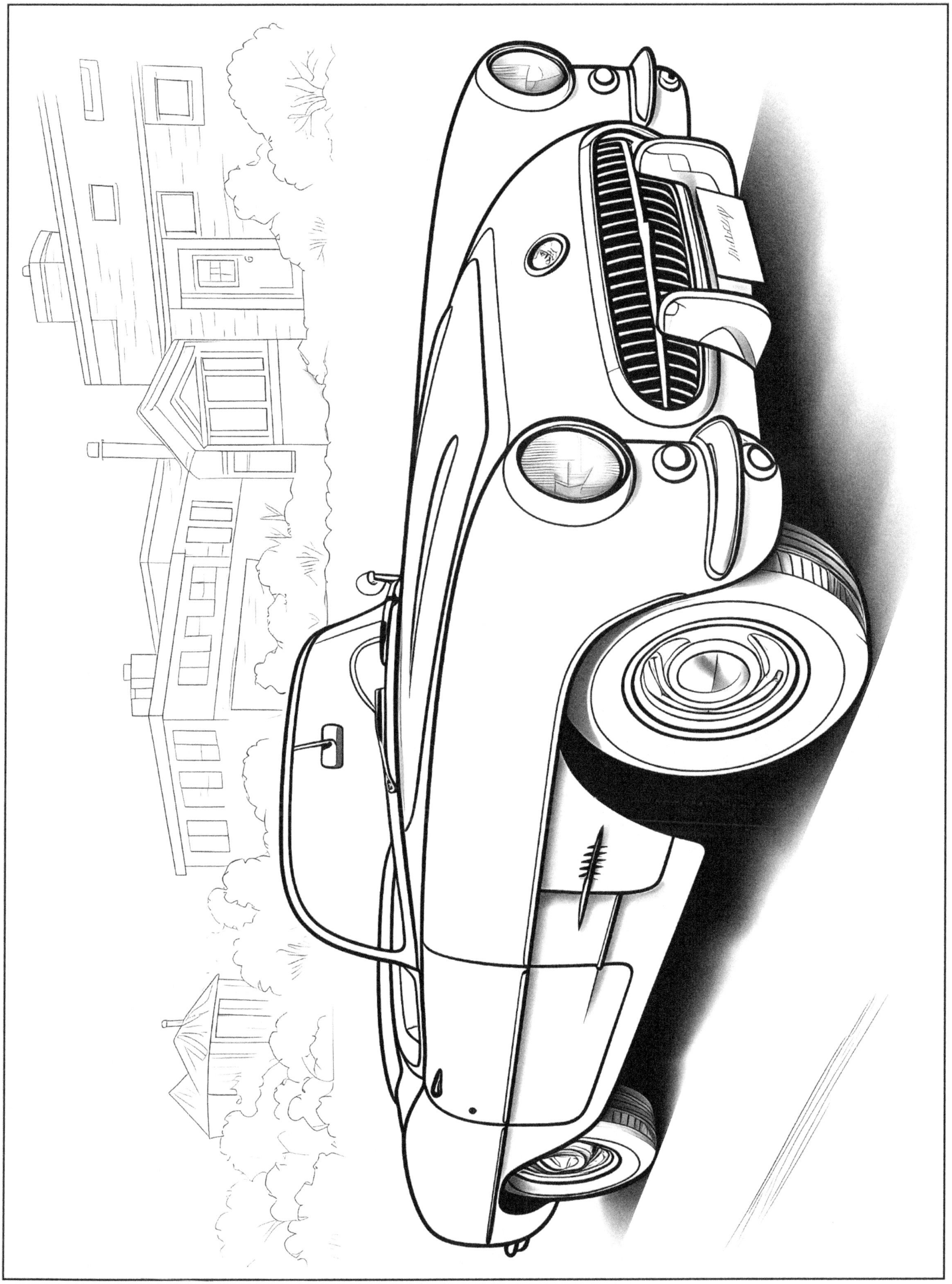

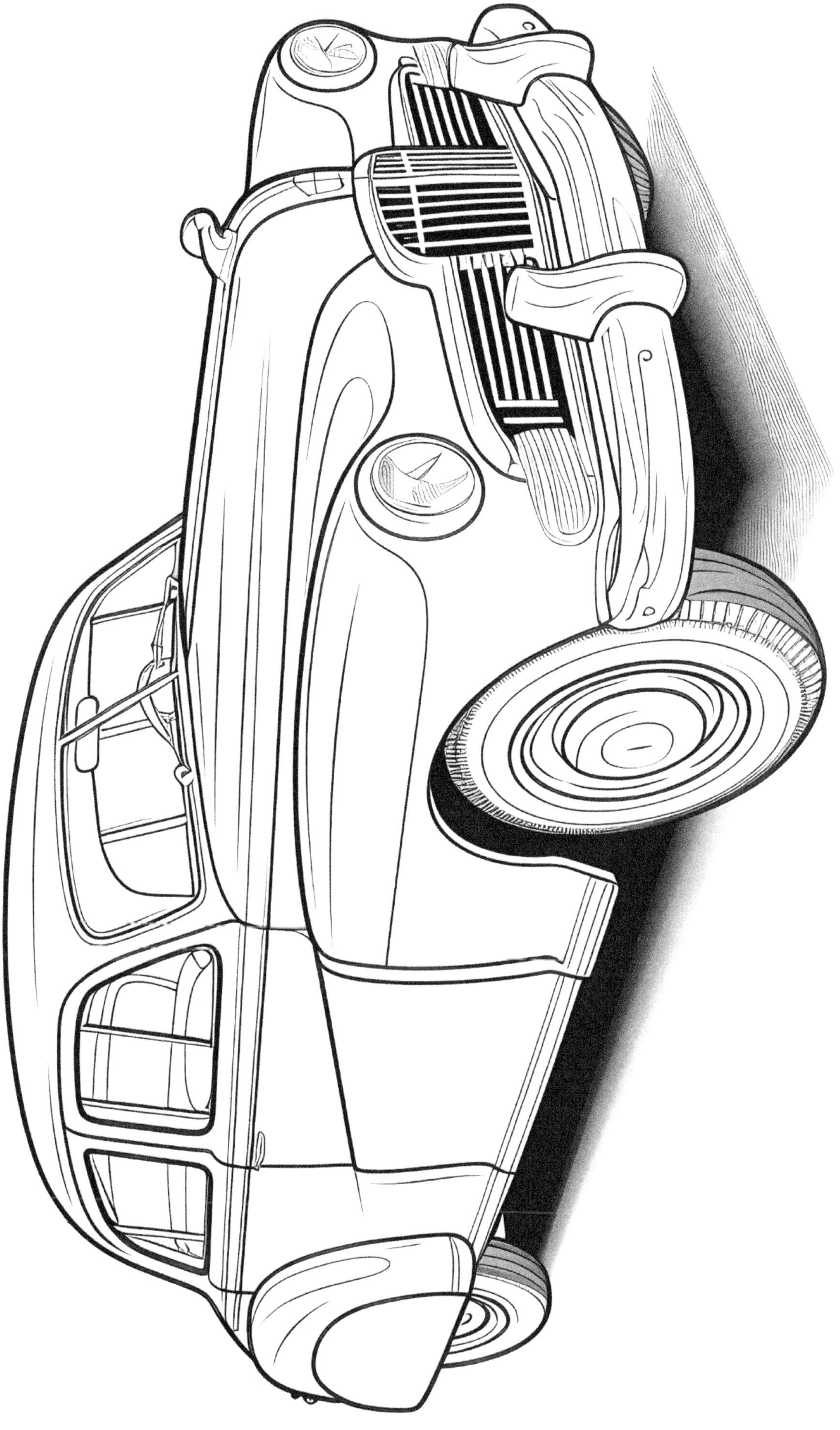

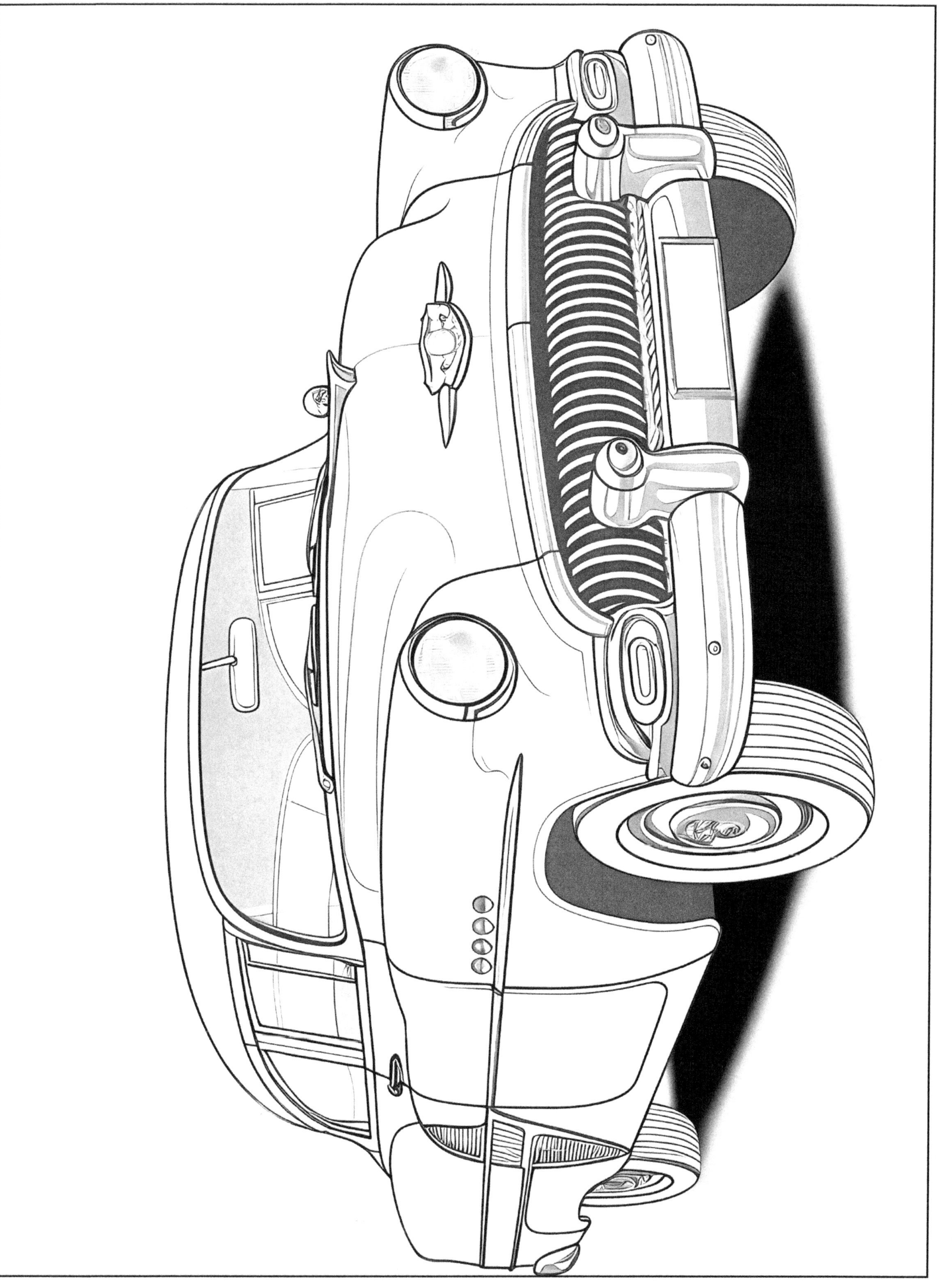

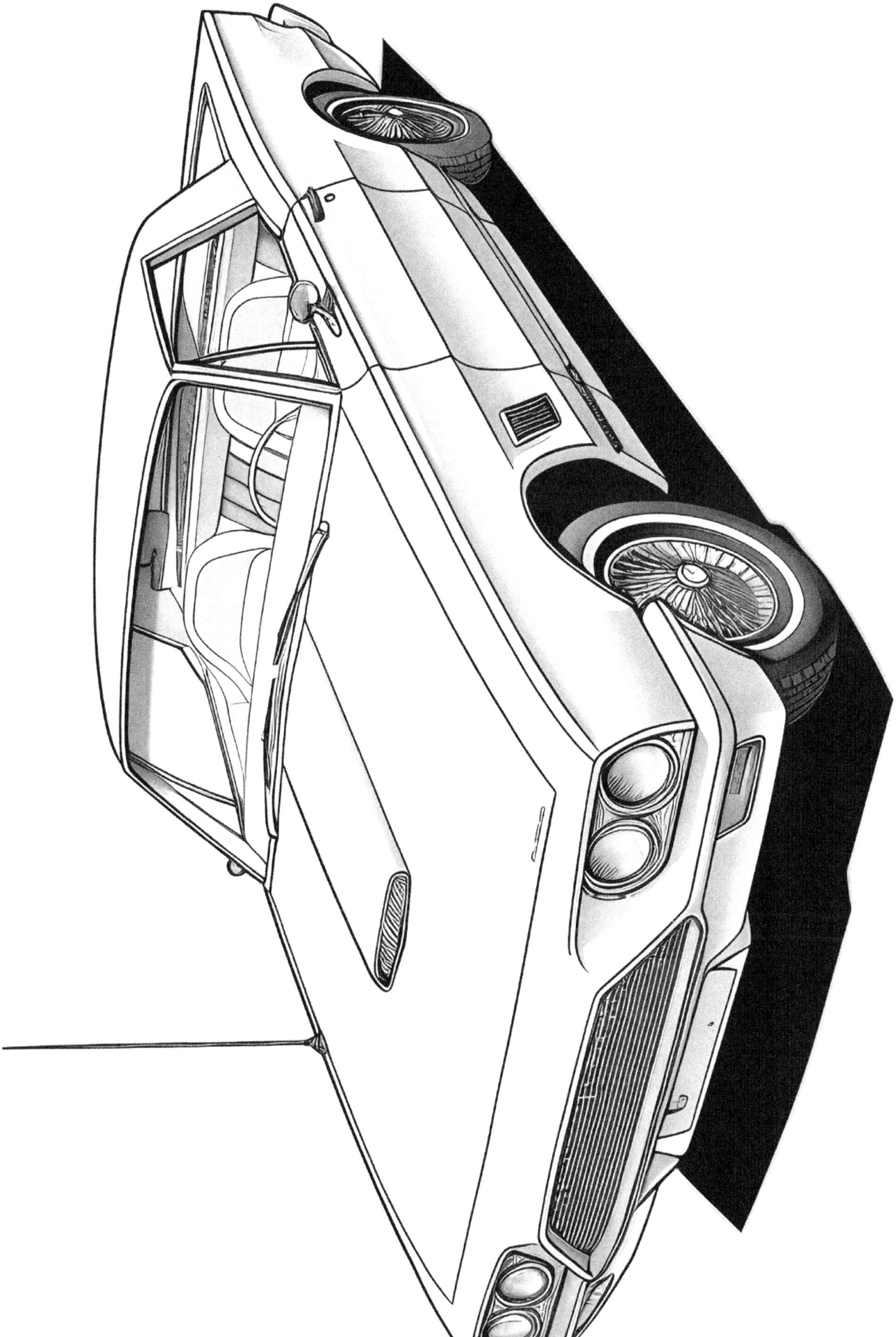

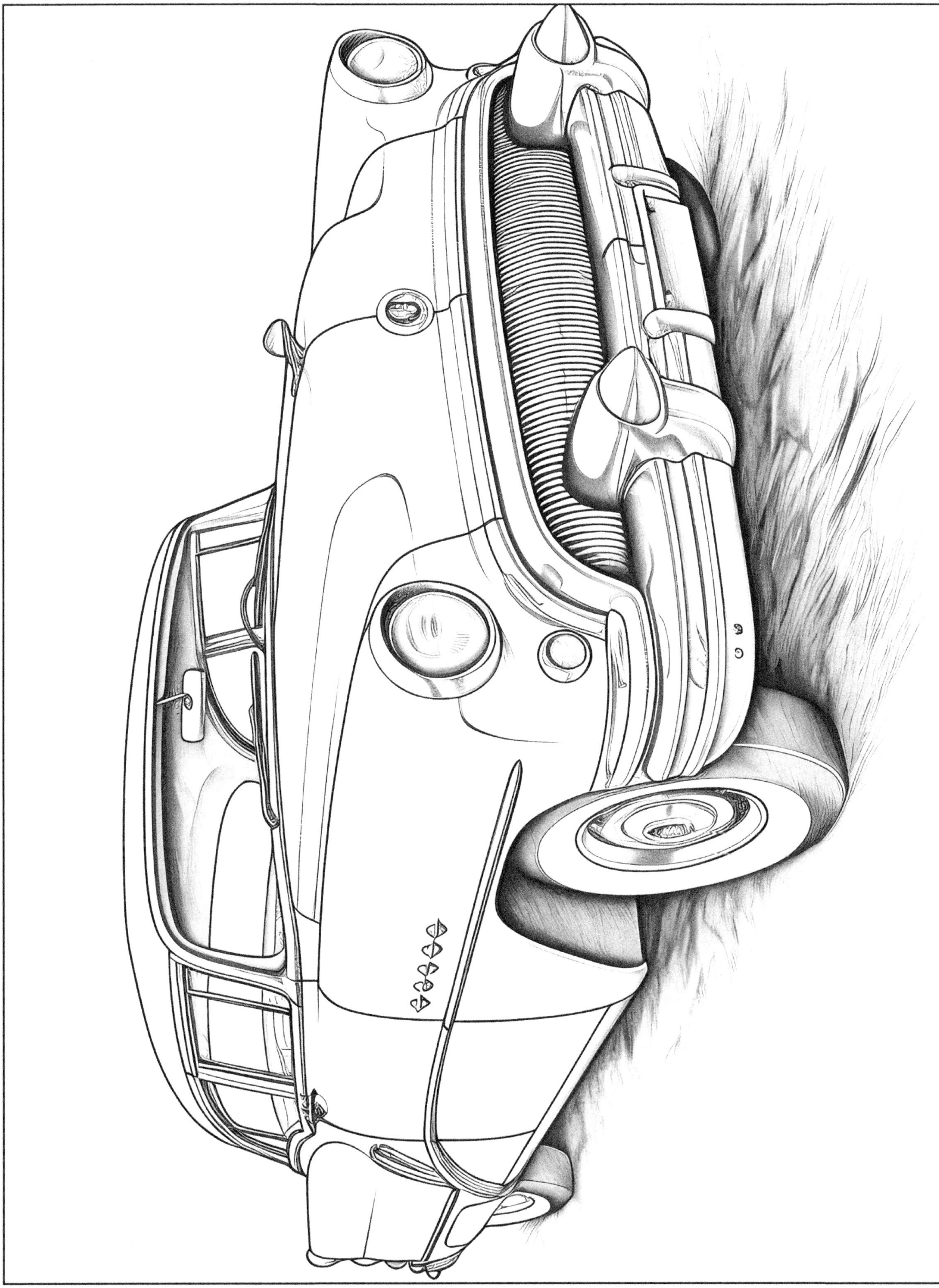

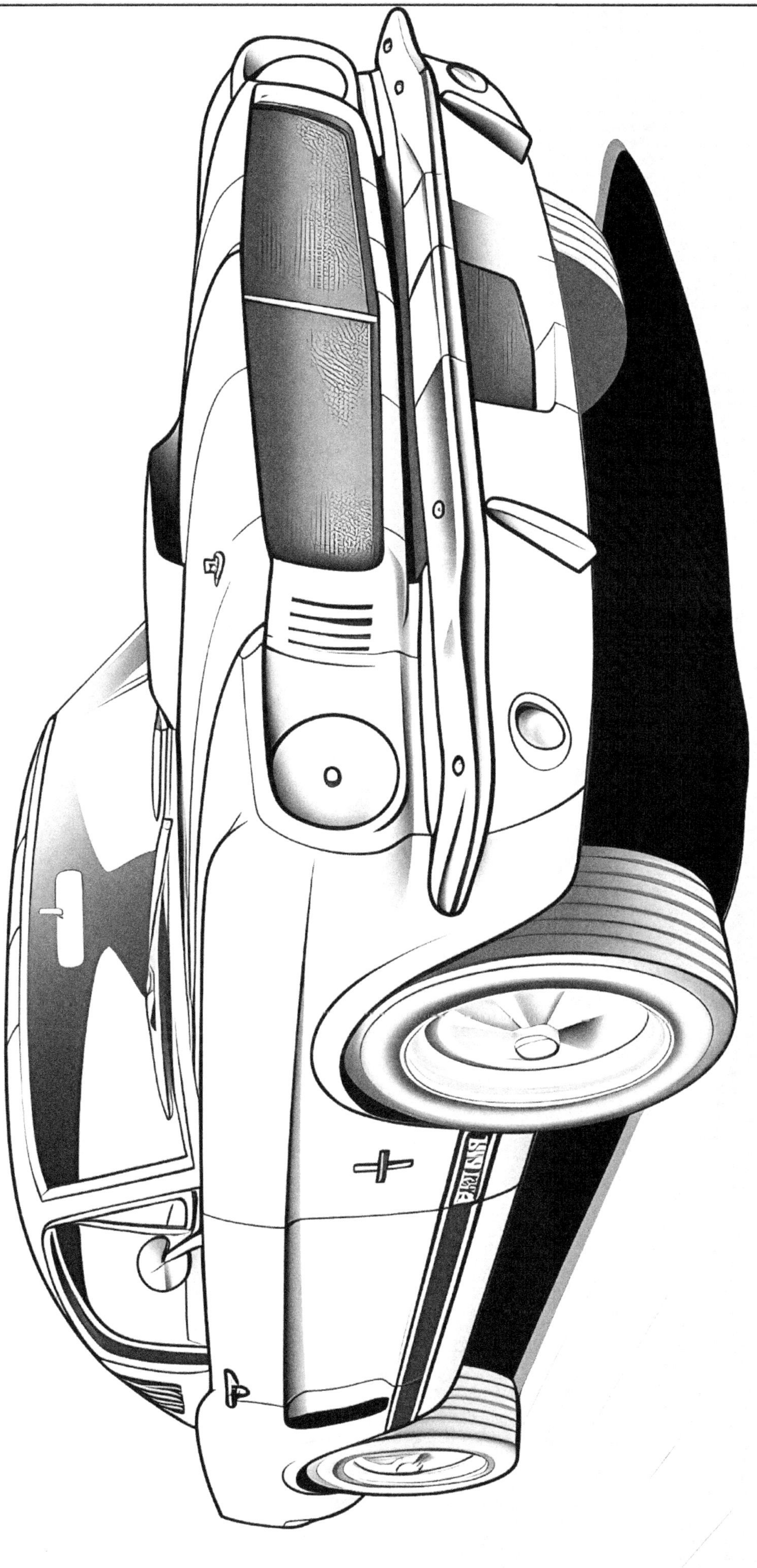

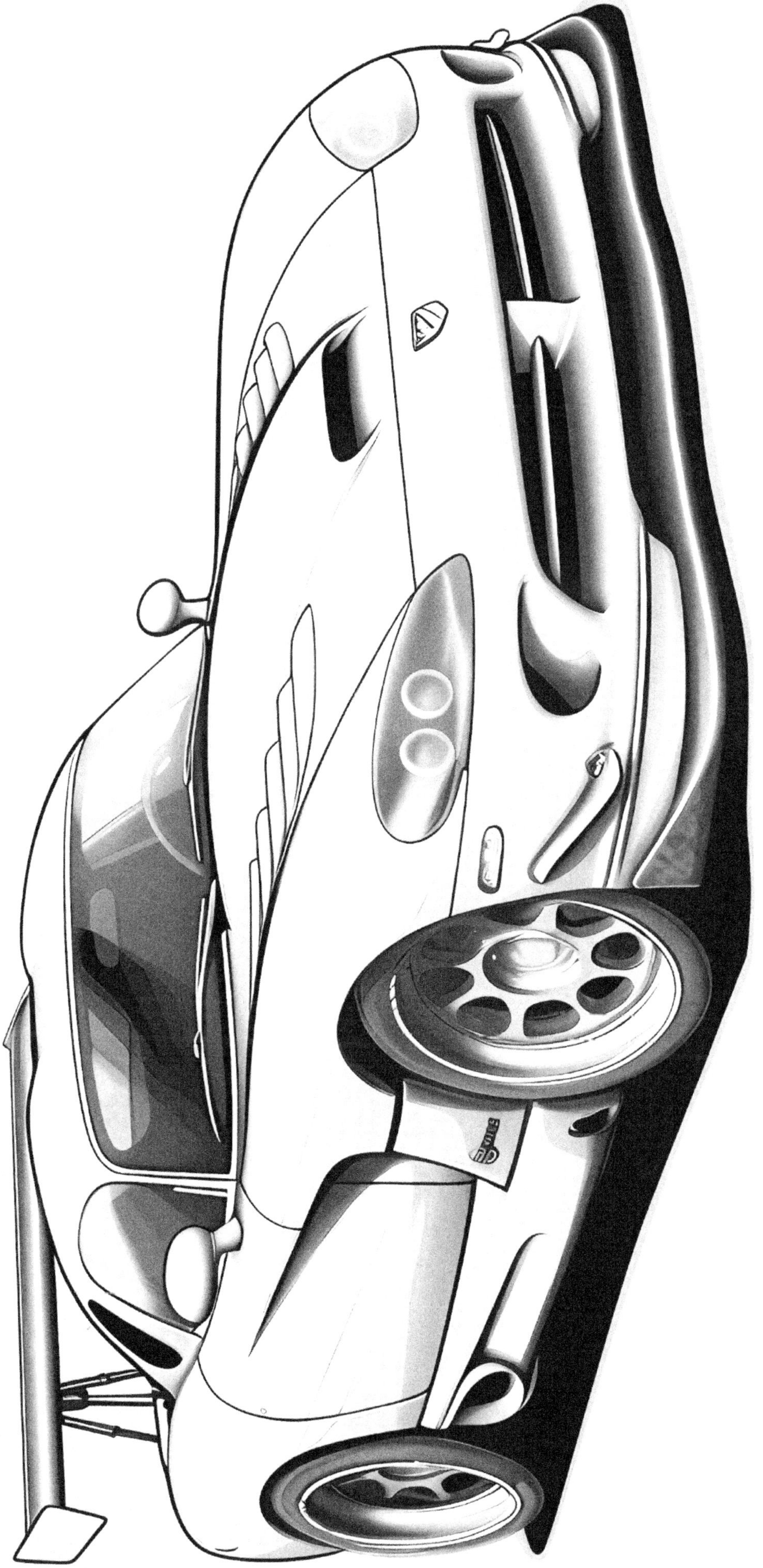

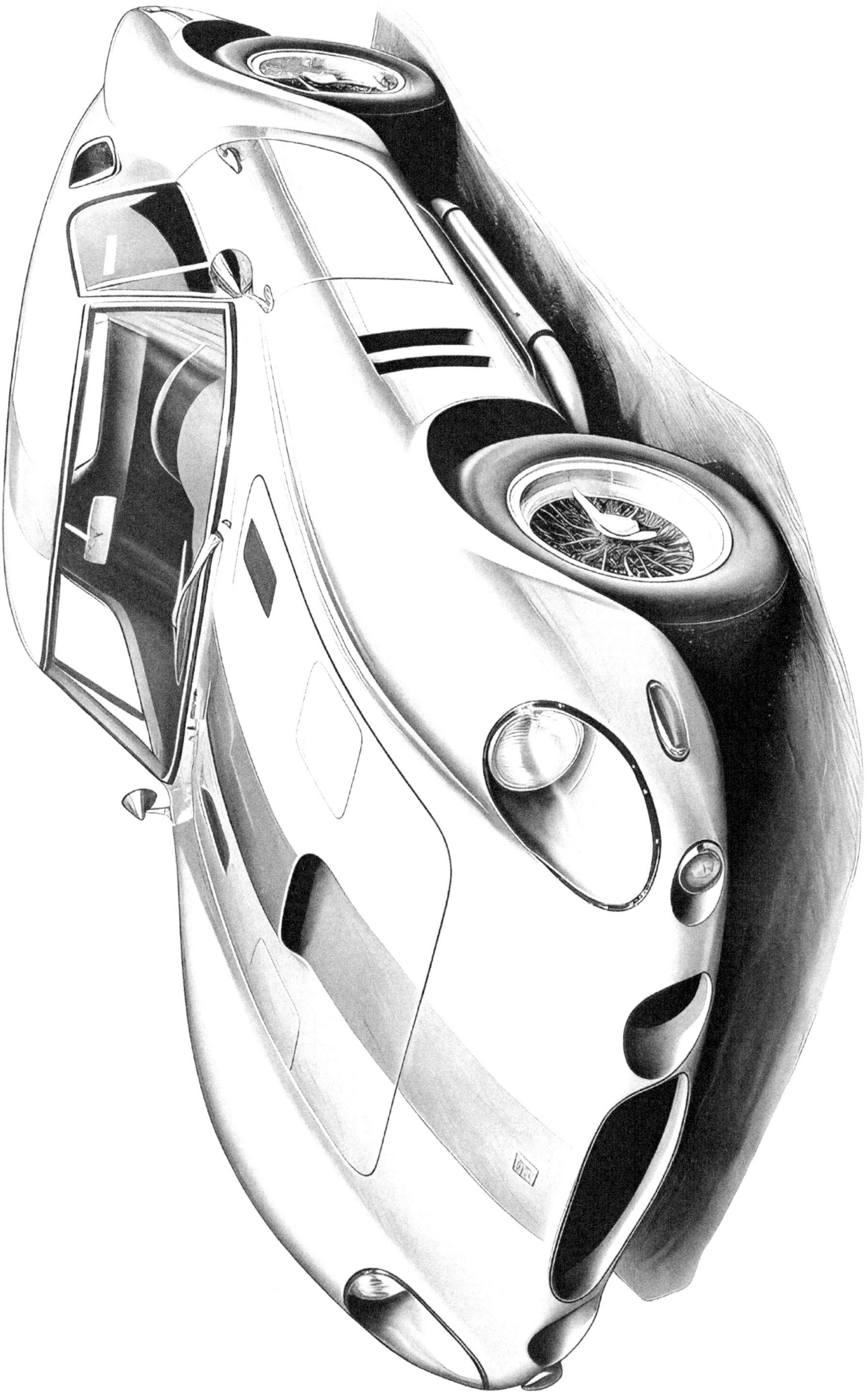

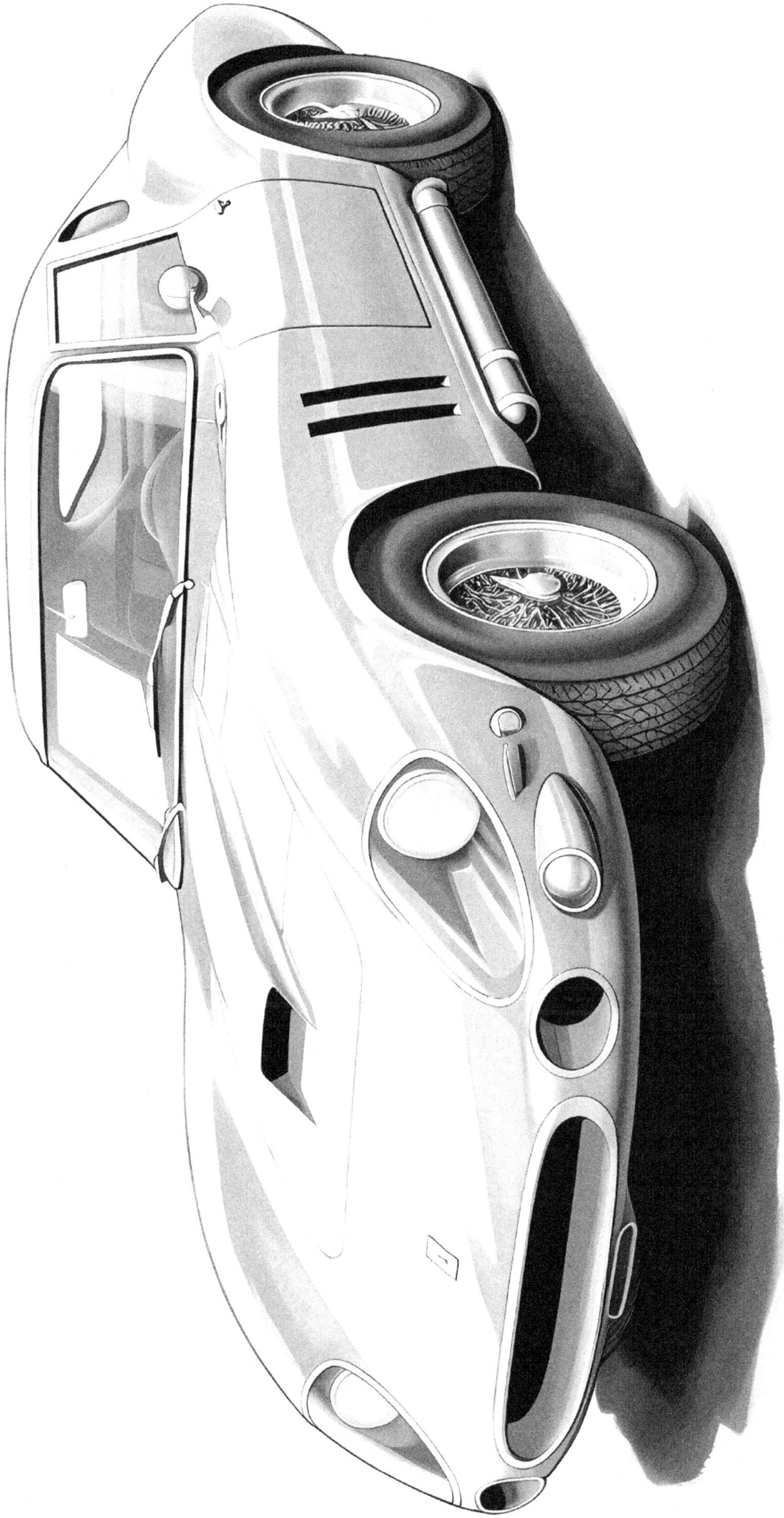

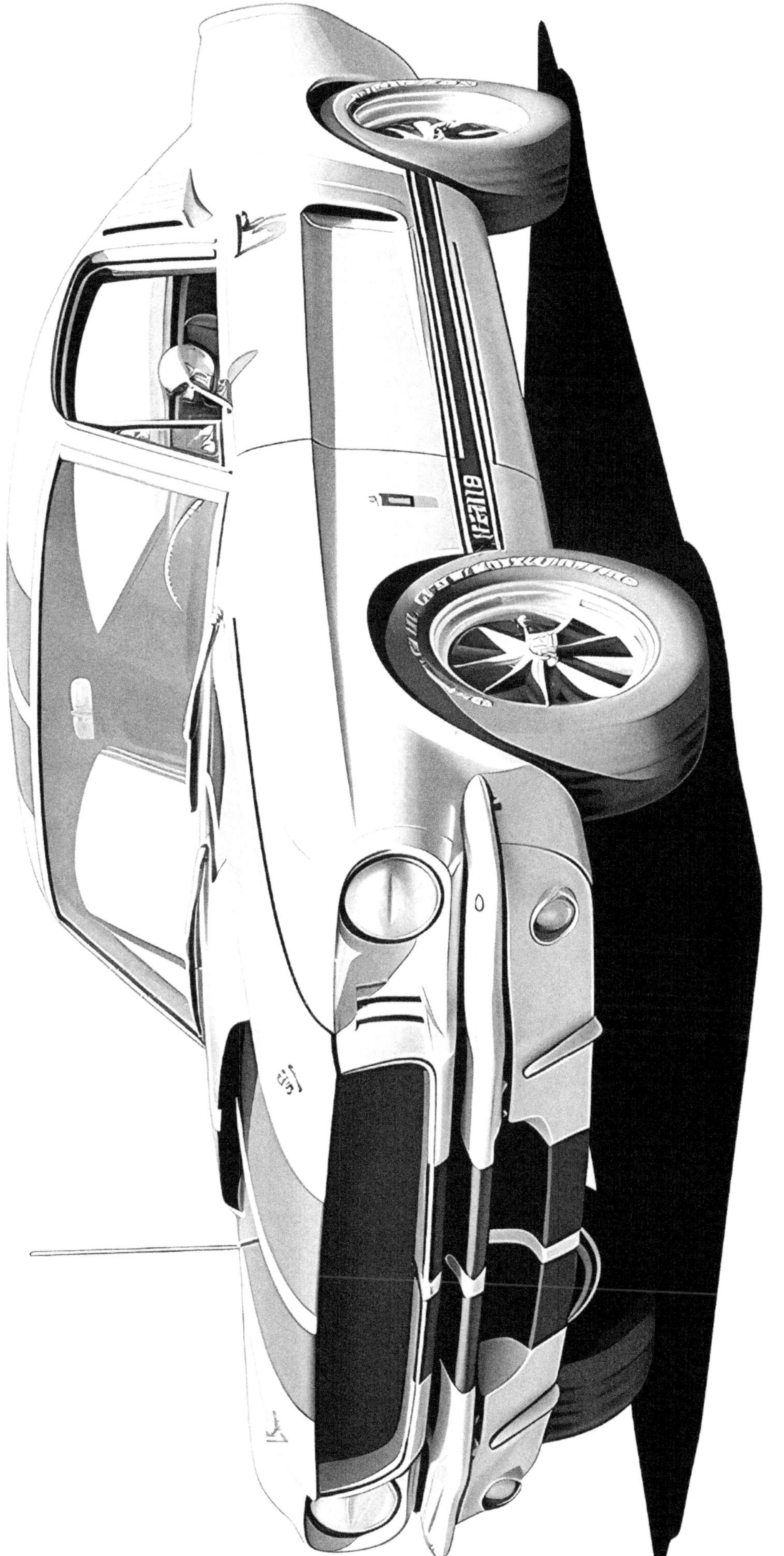

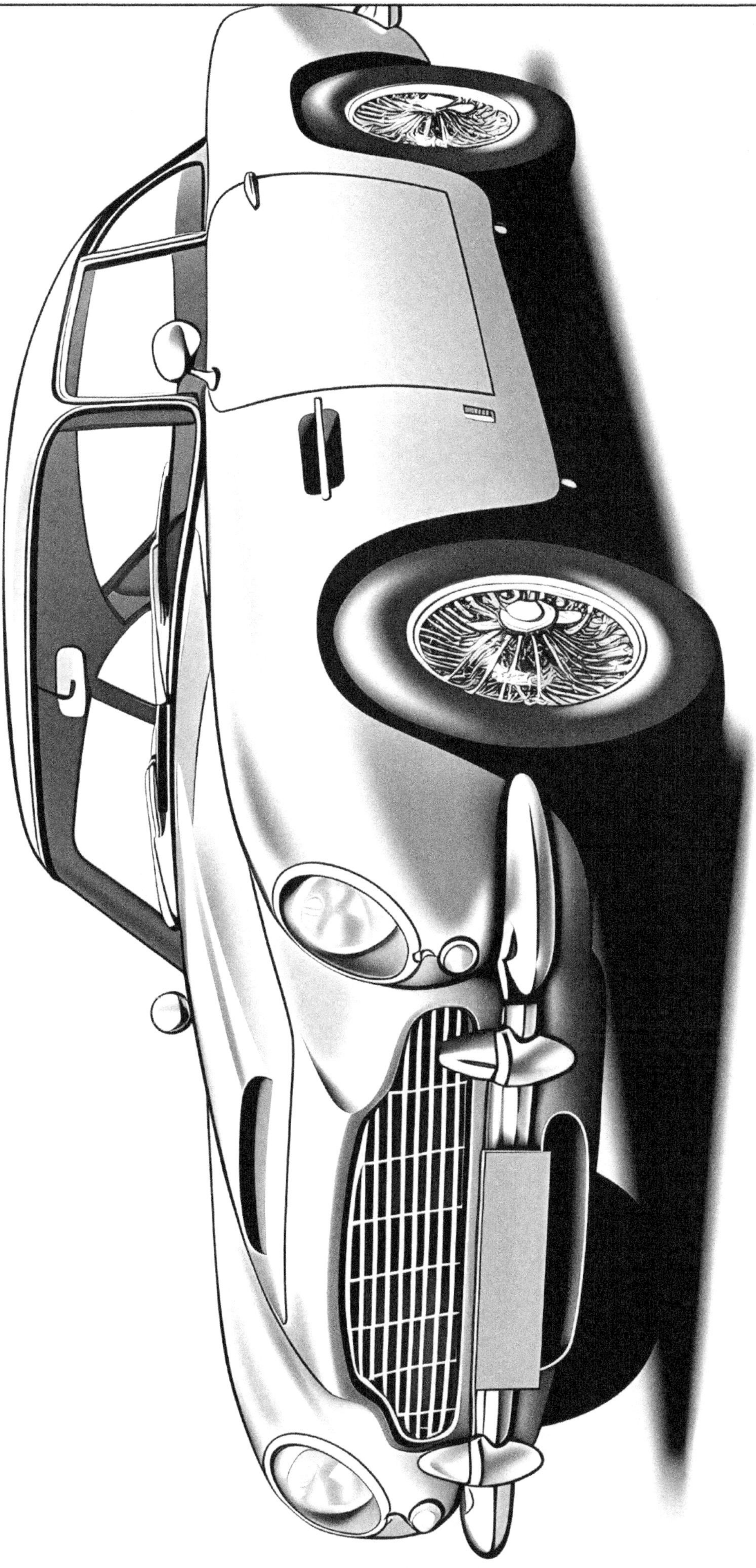

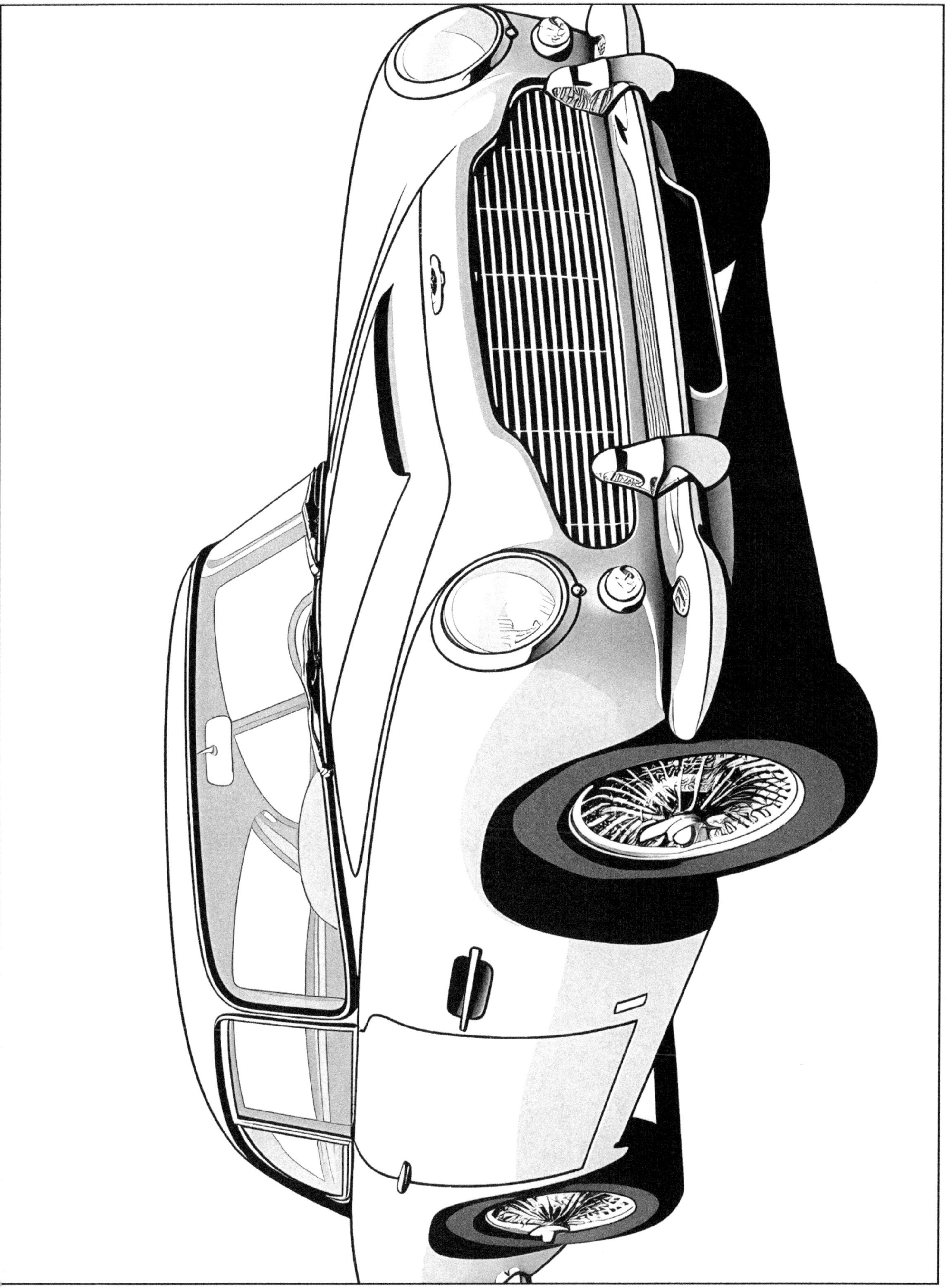

NC8 C1CZ

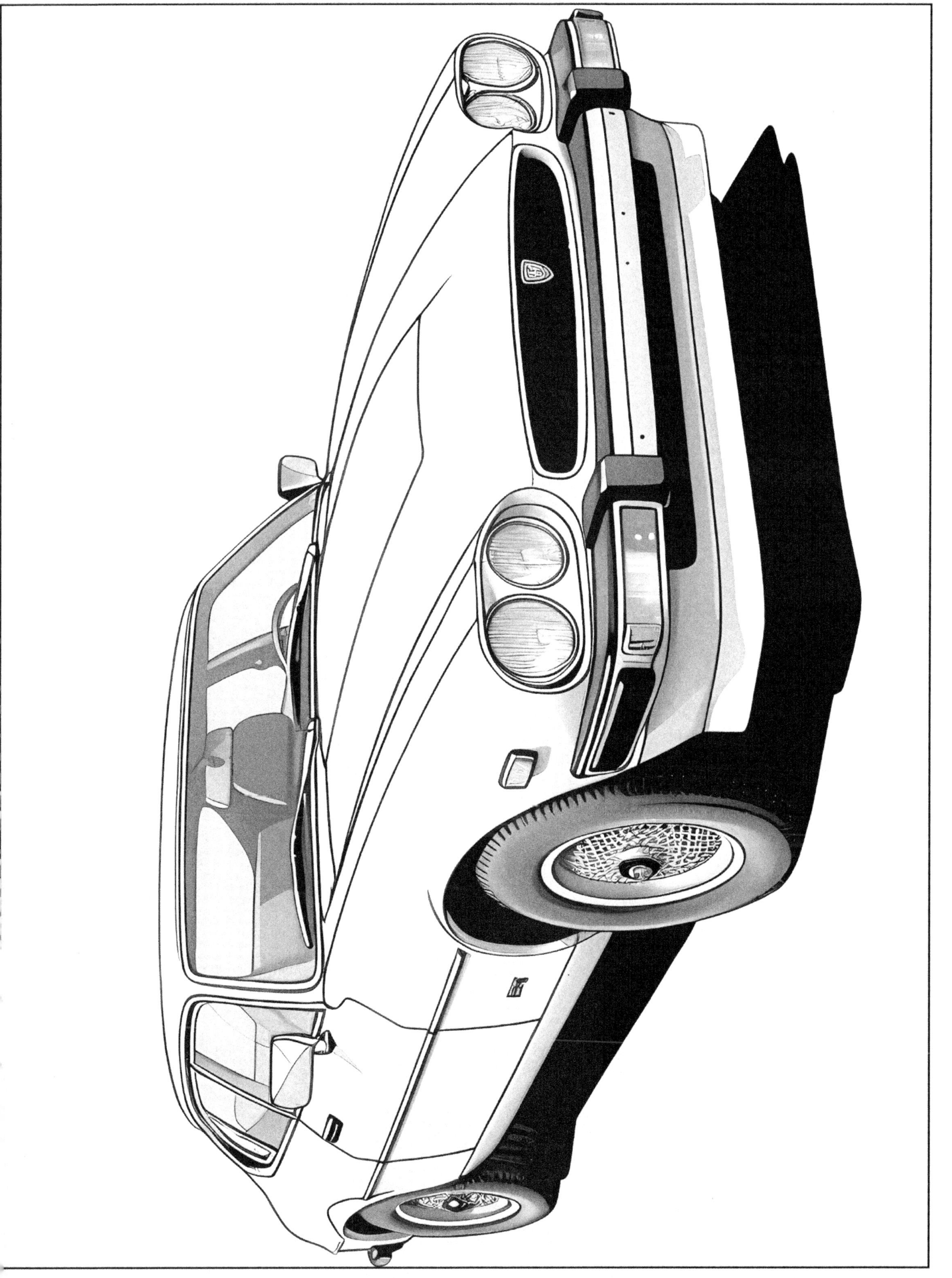

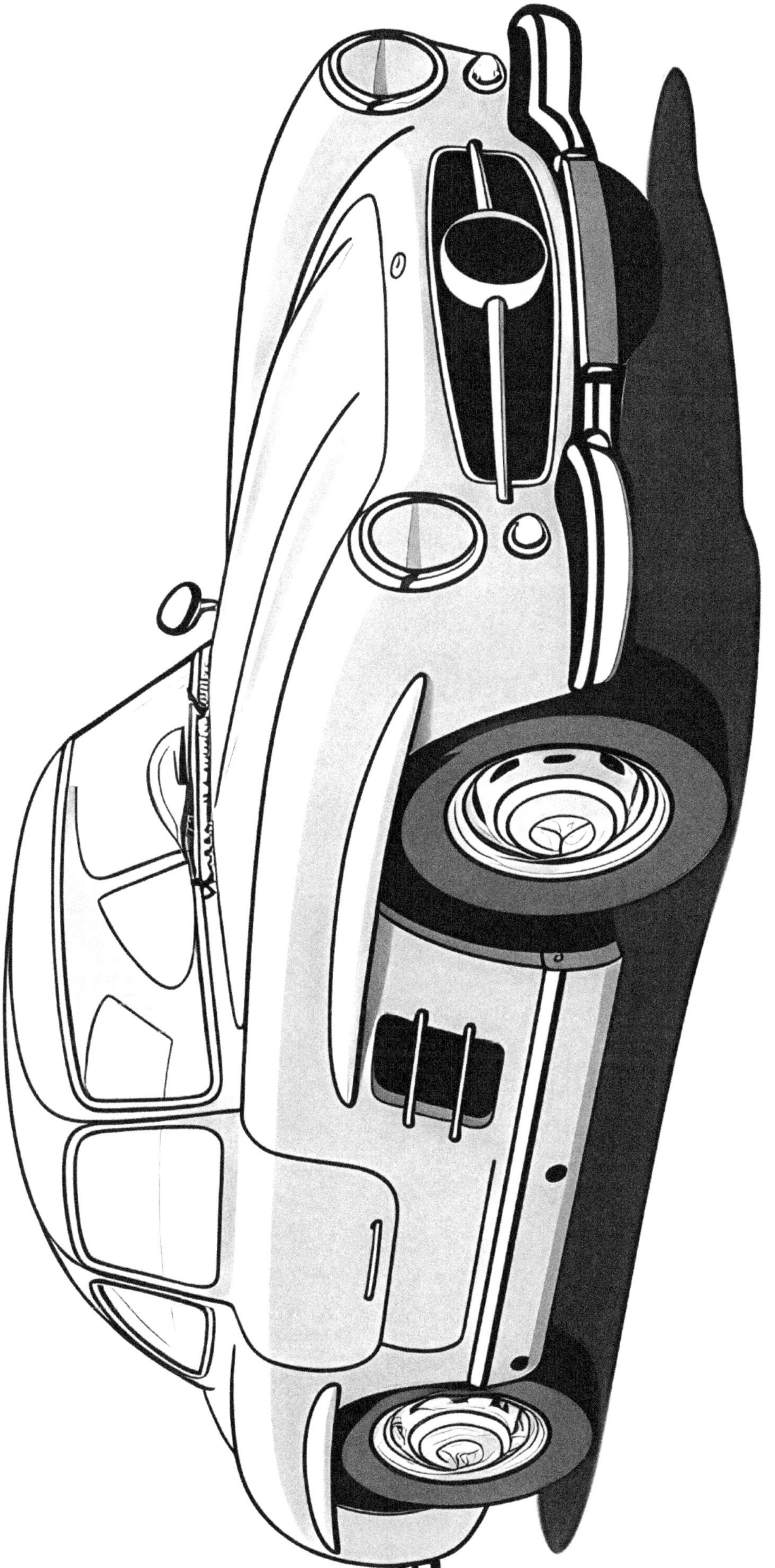

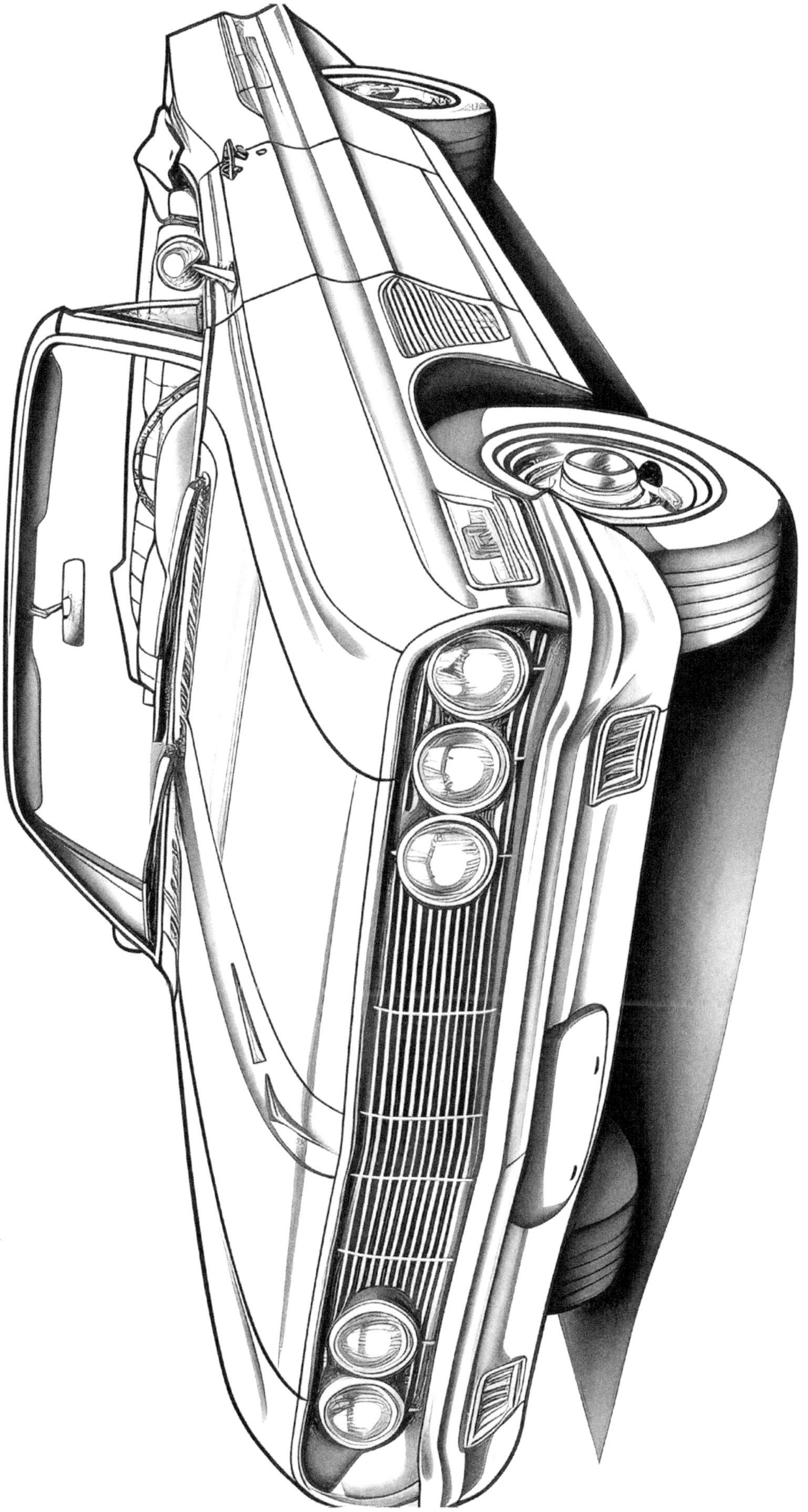

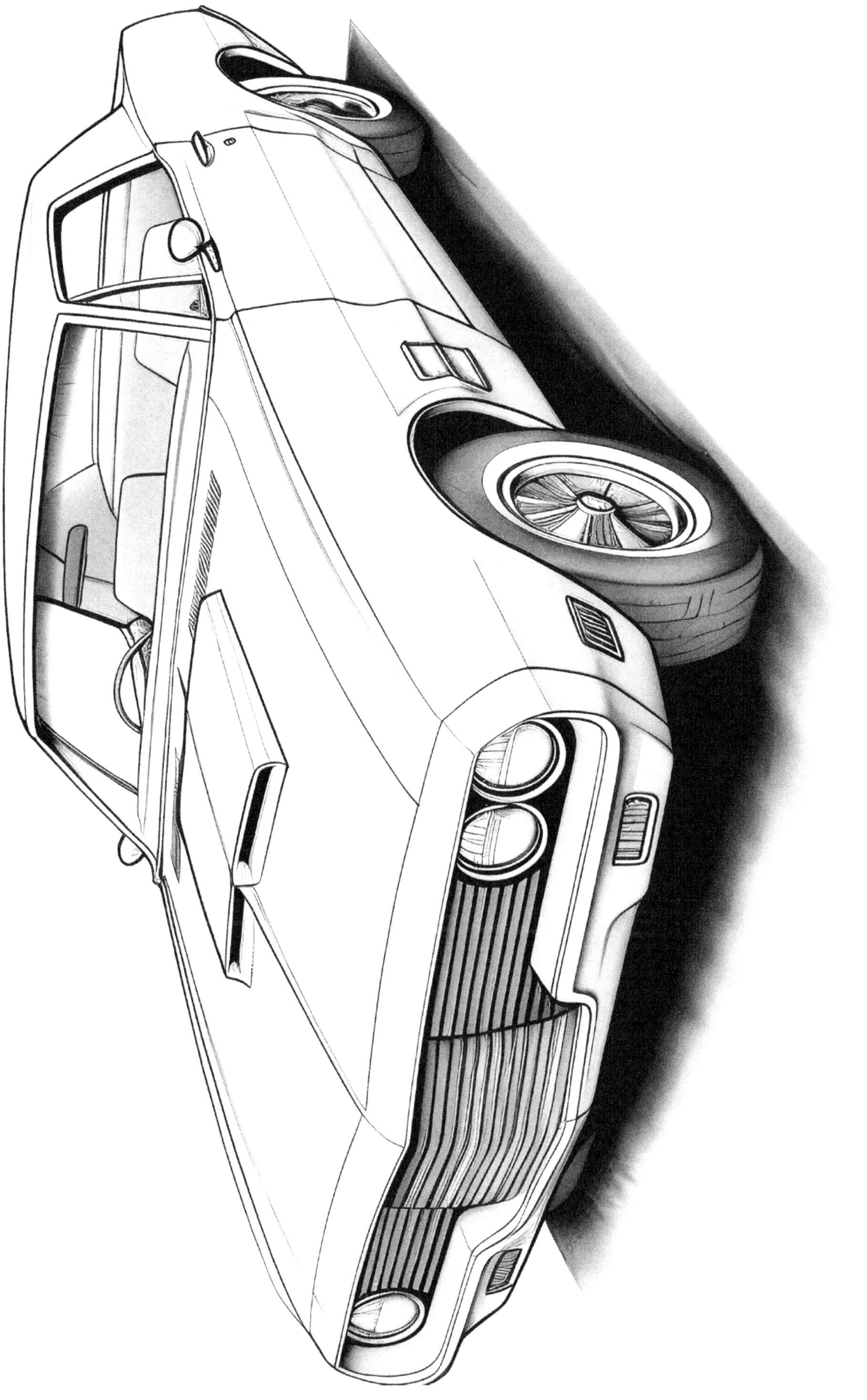

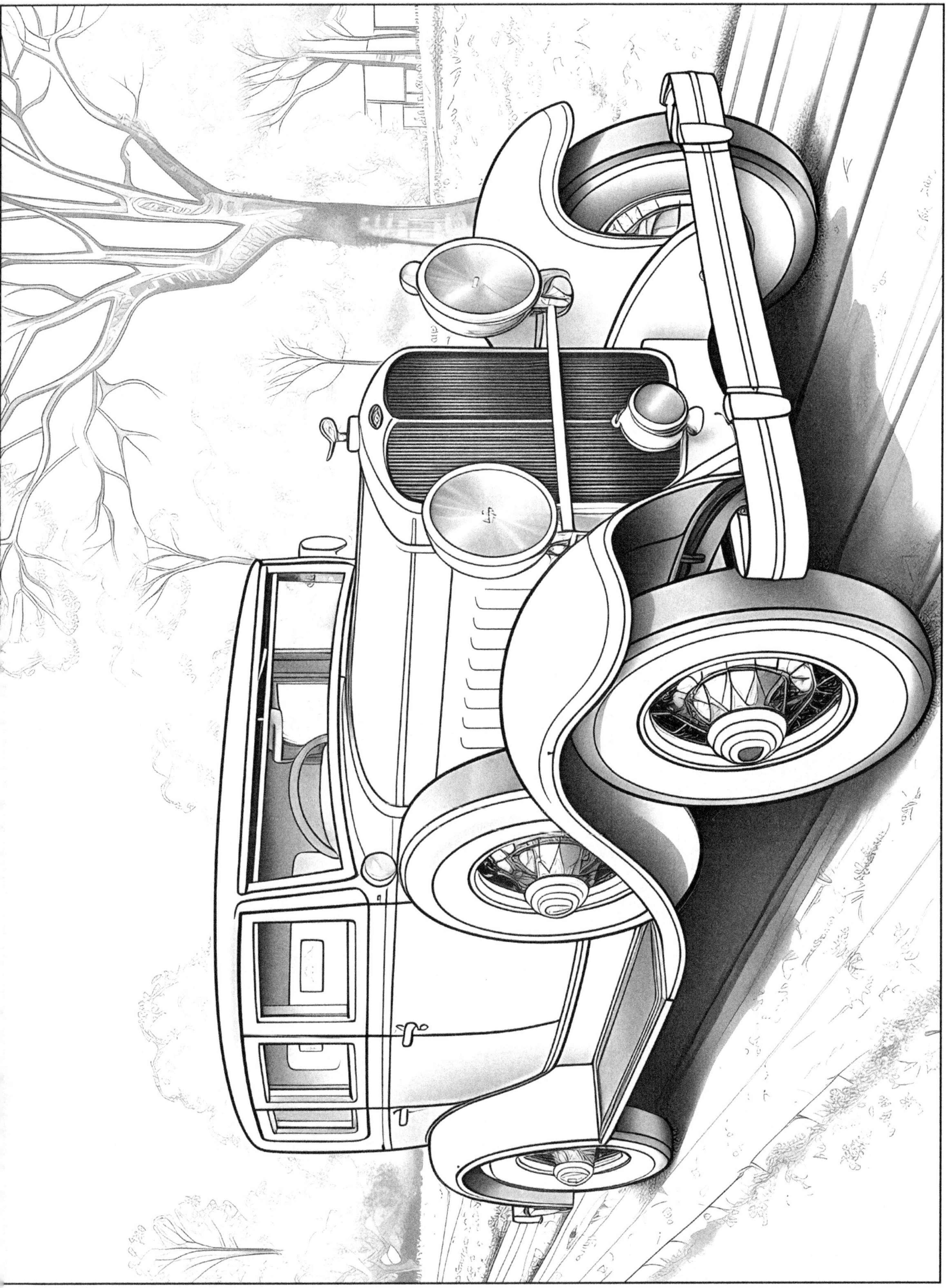

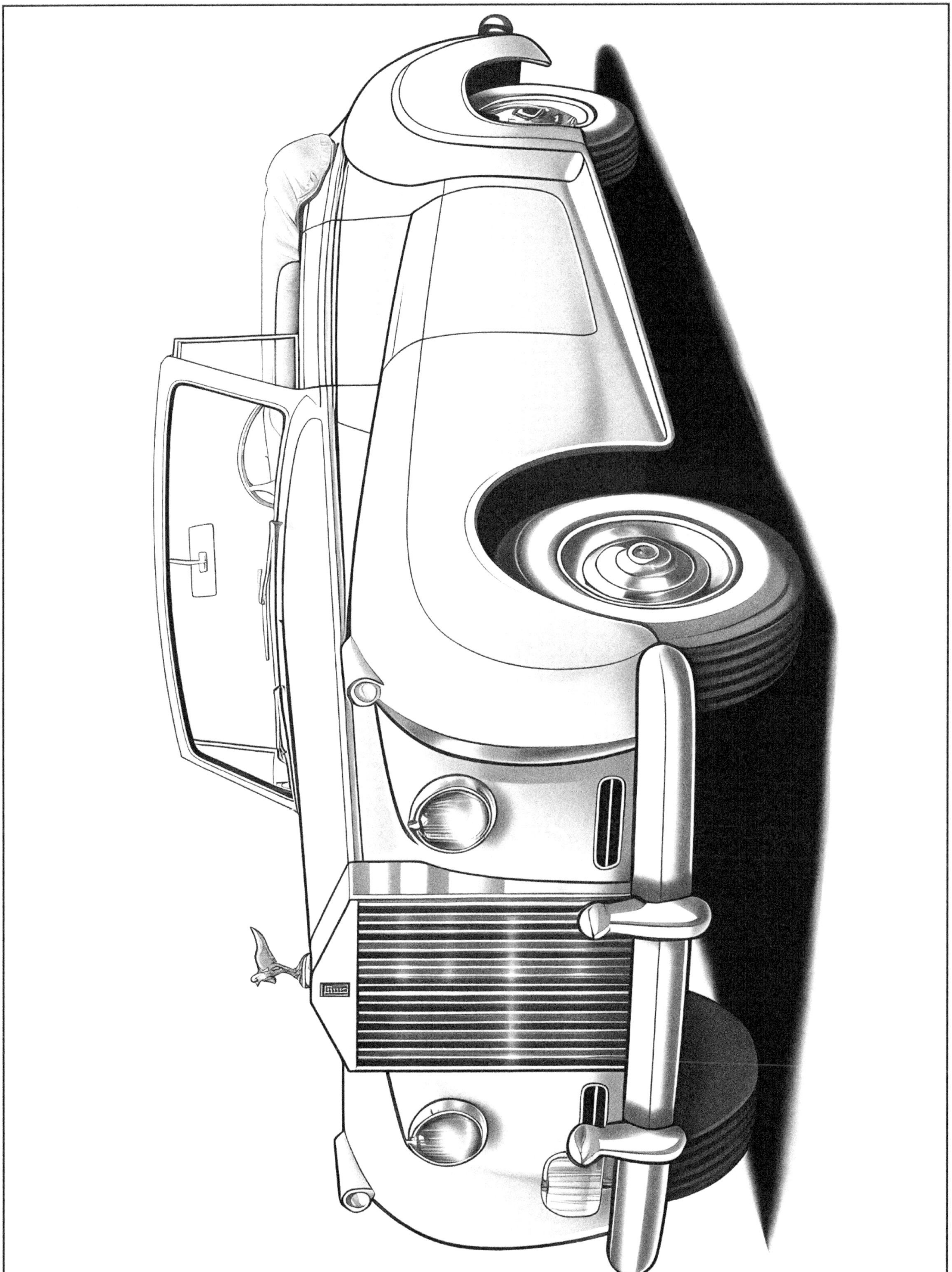

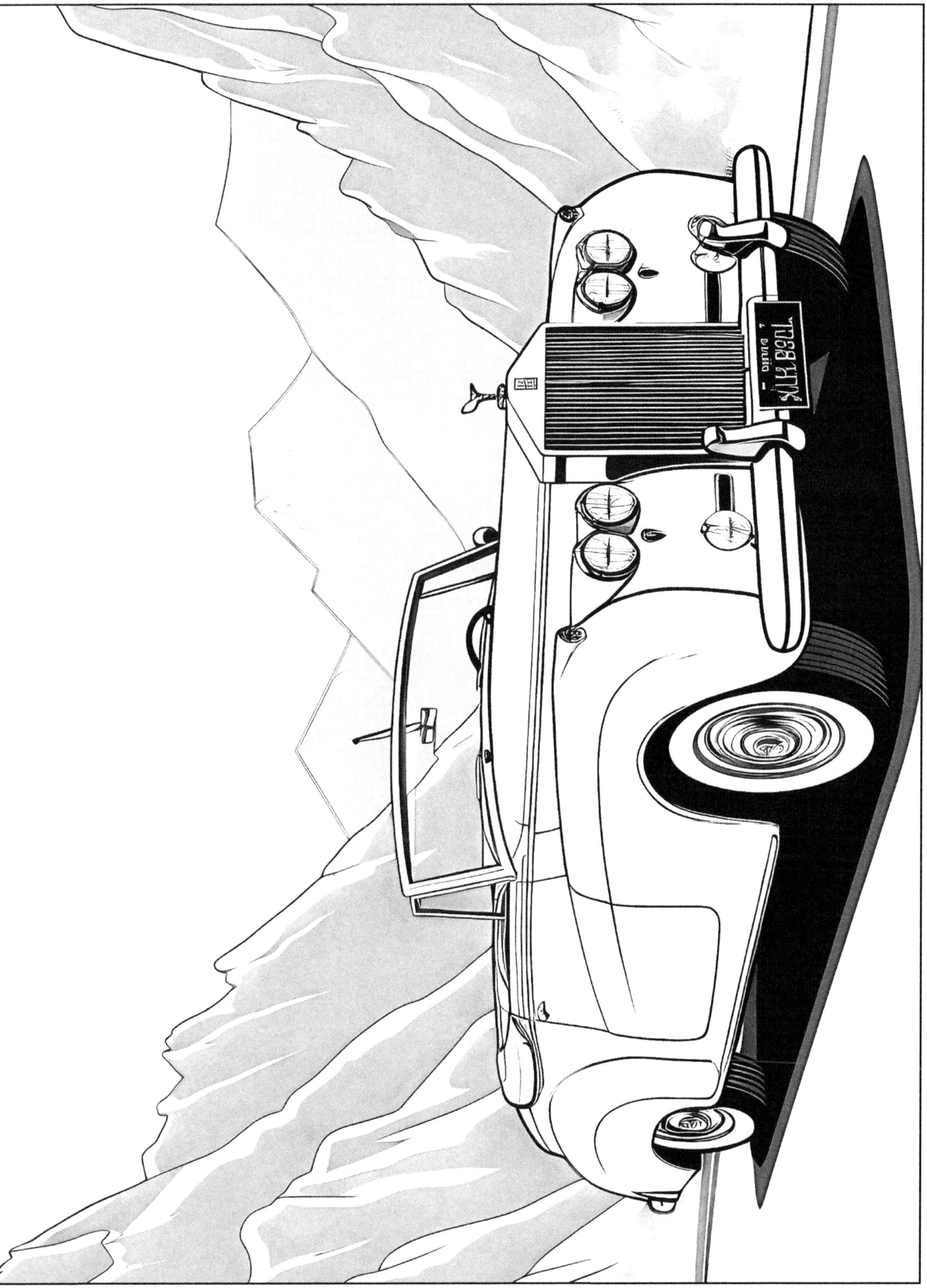

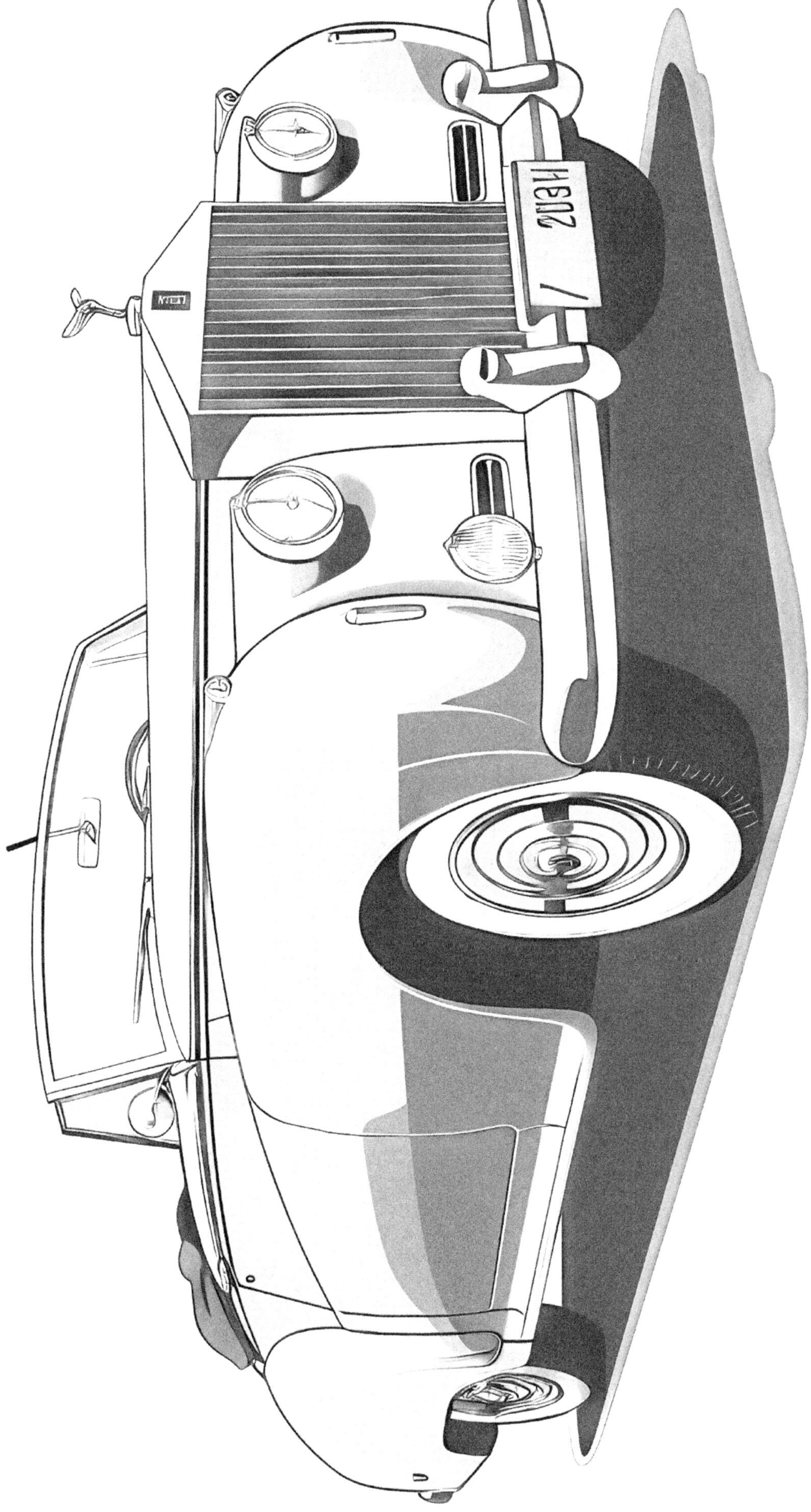

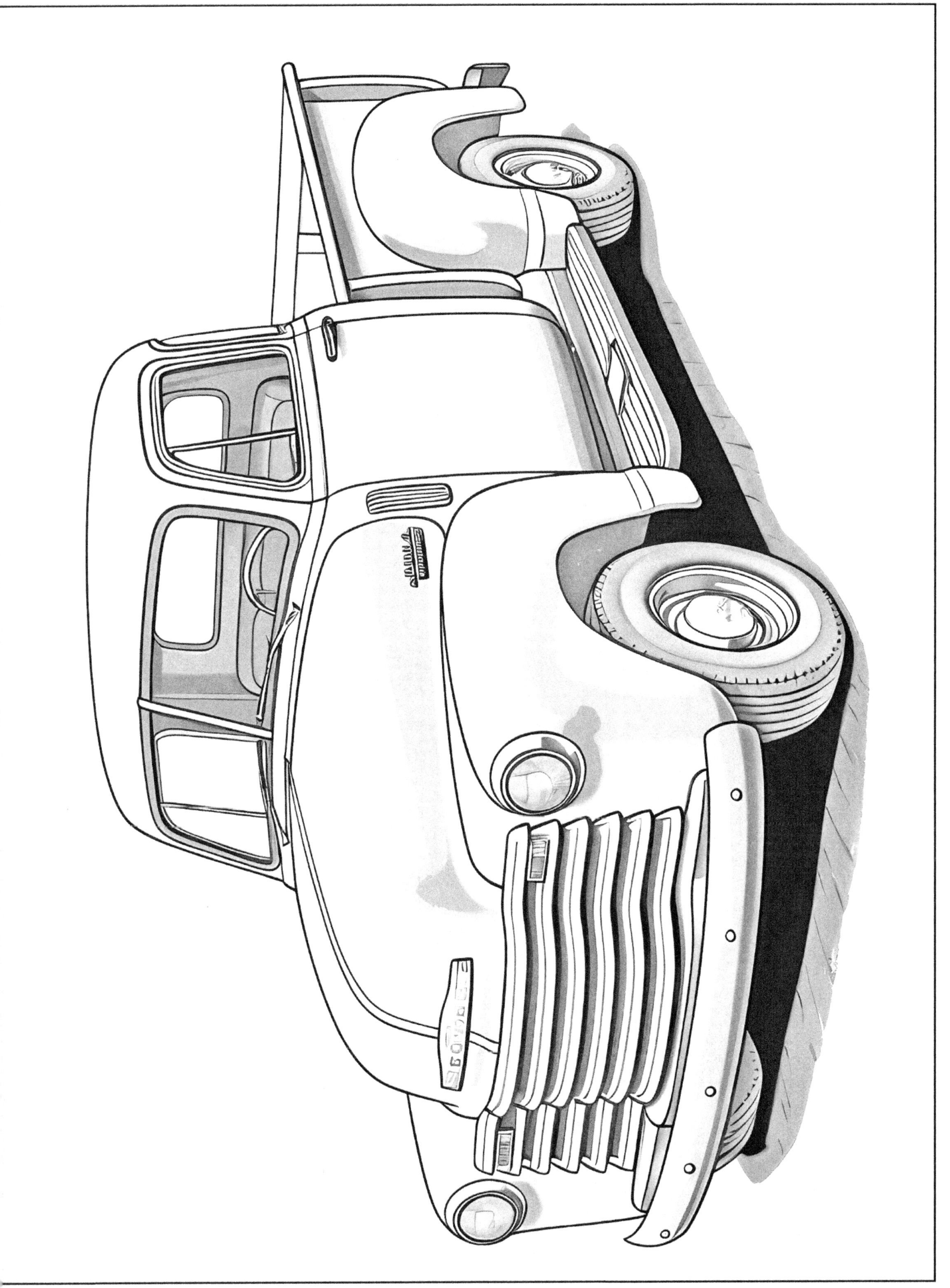

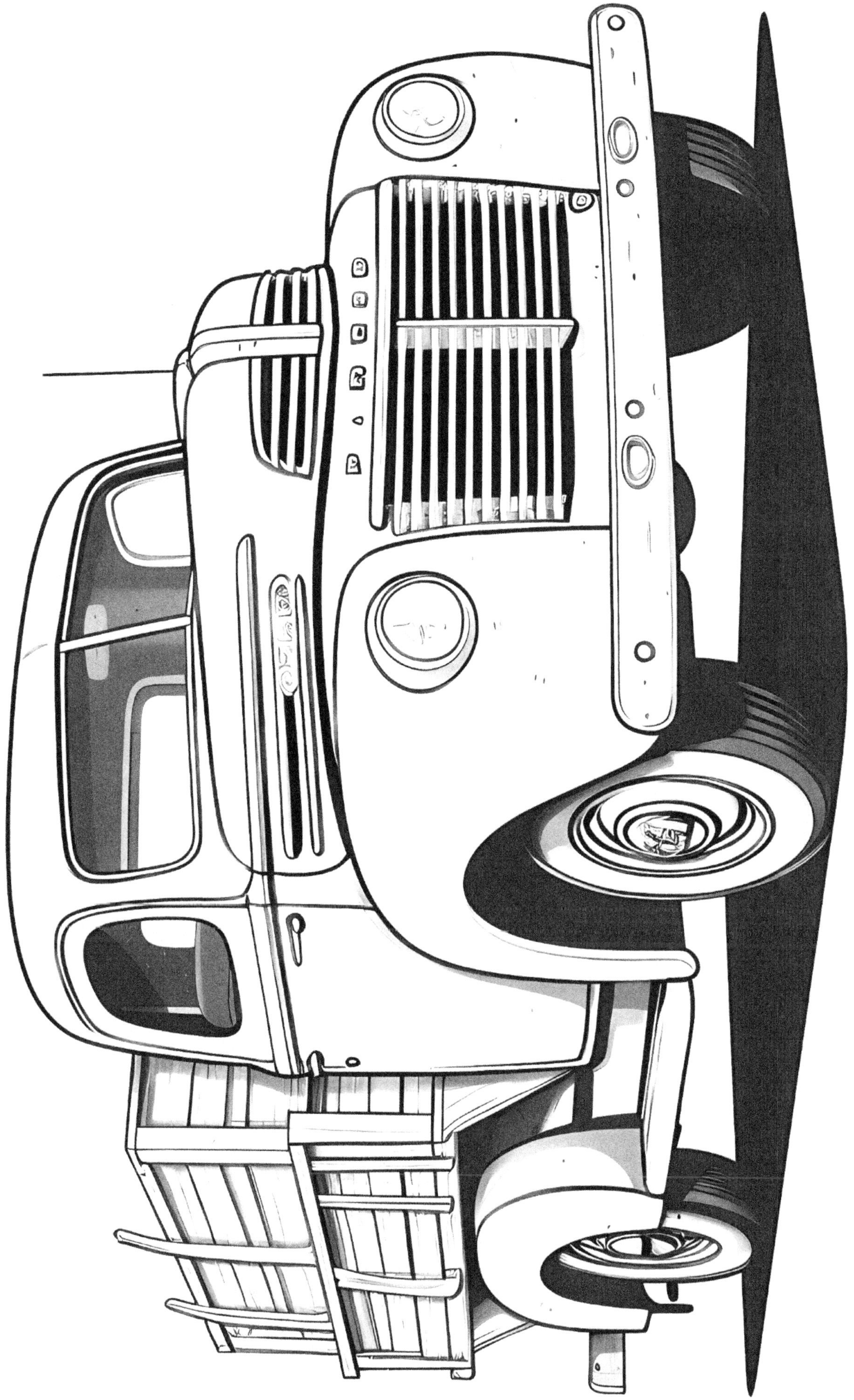

LMC

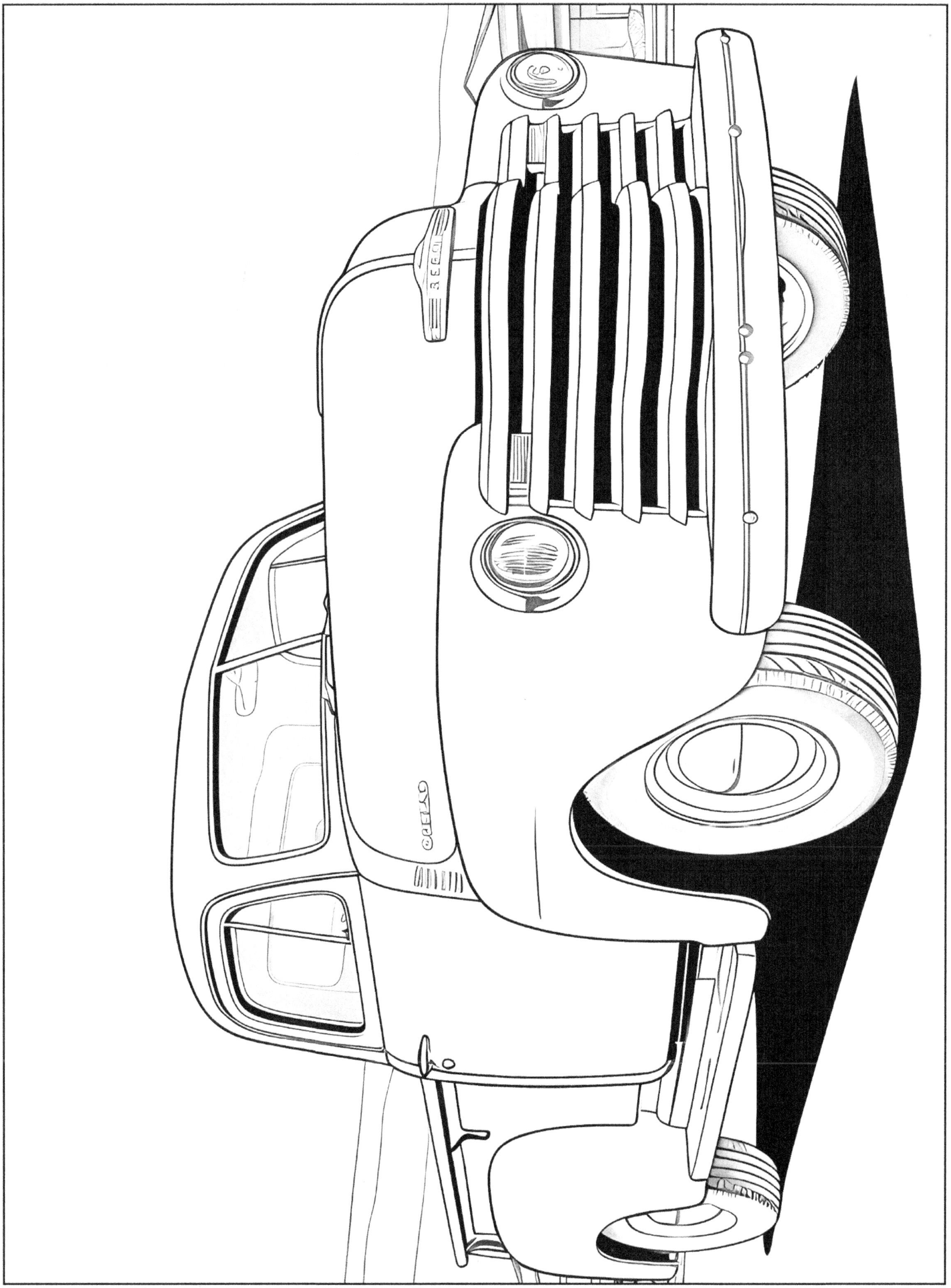

CTJ

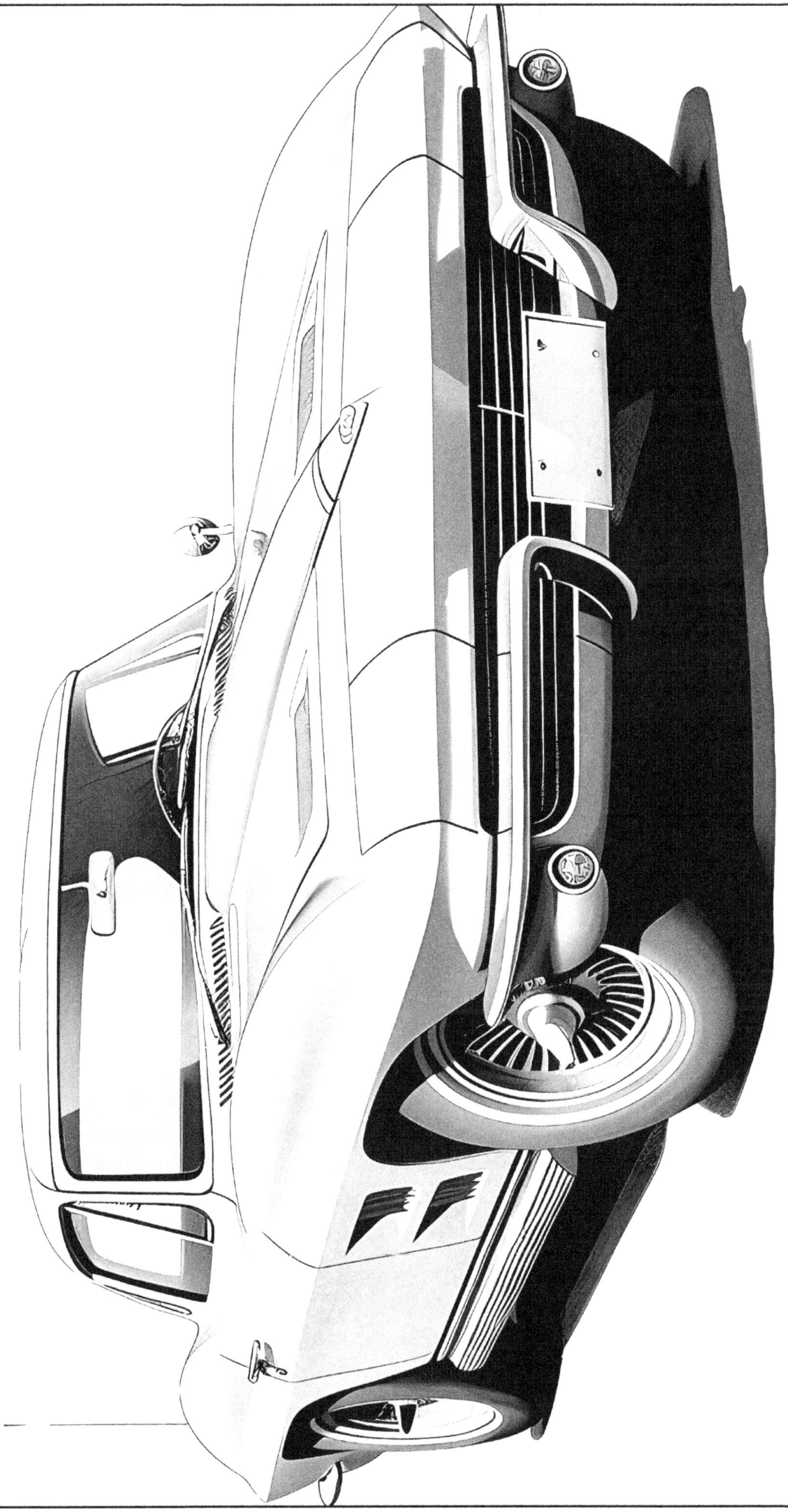

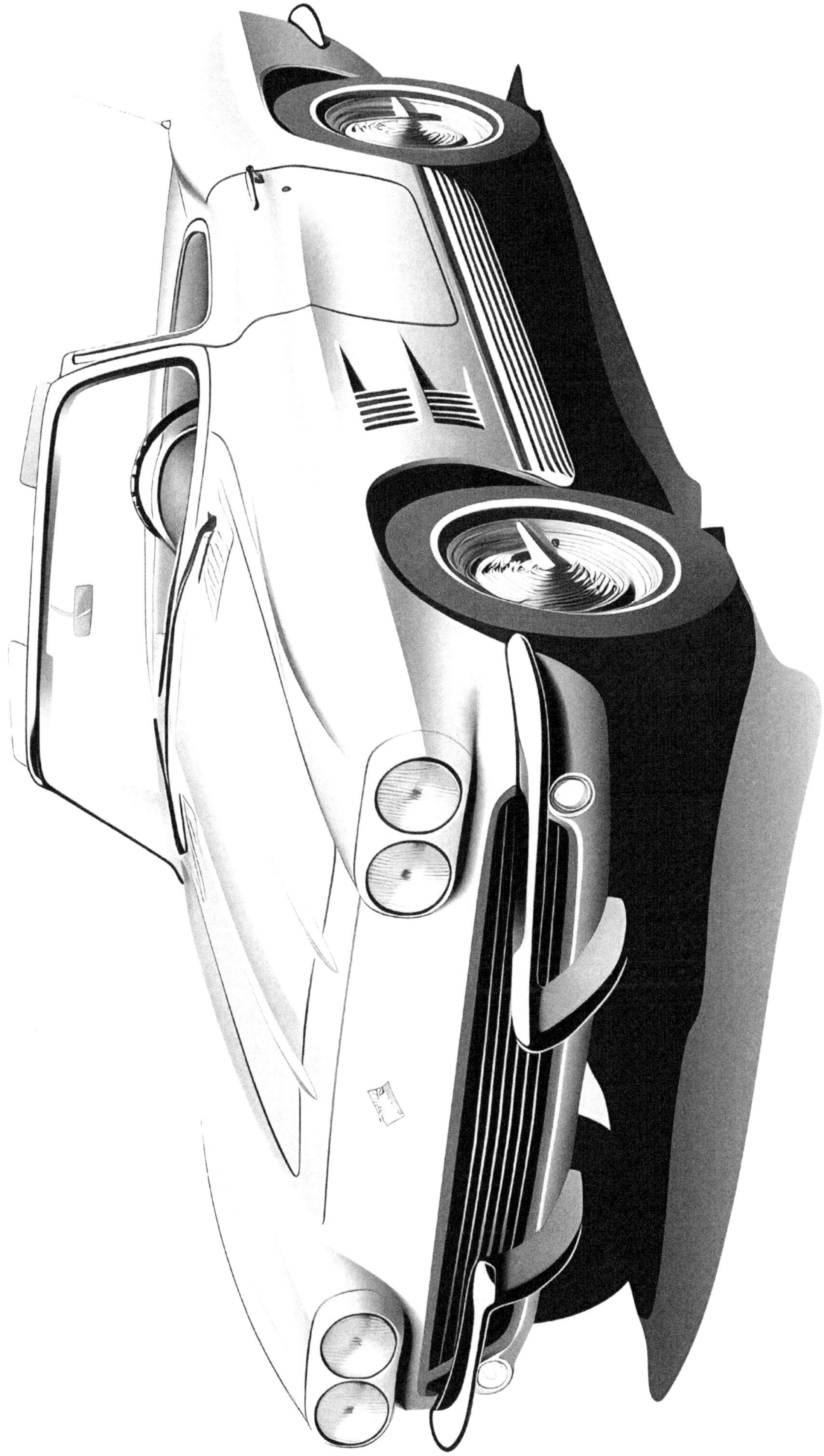

SS

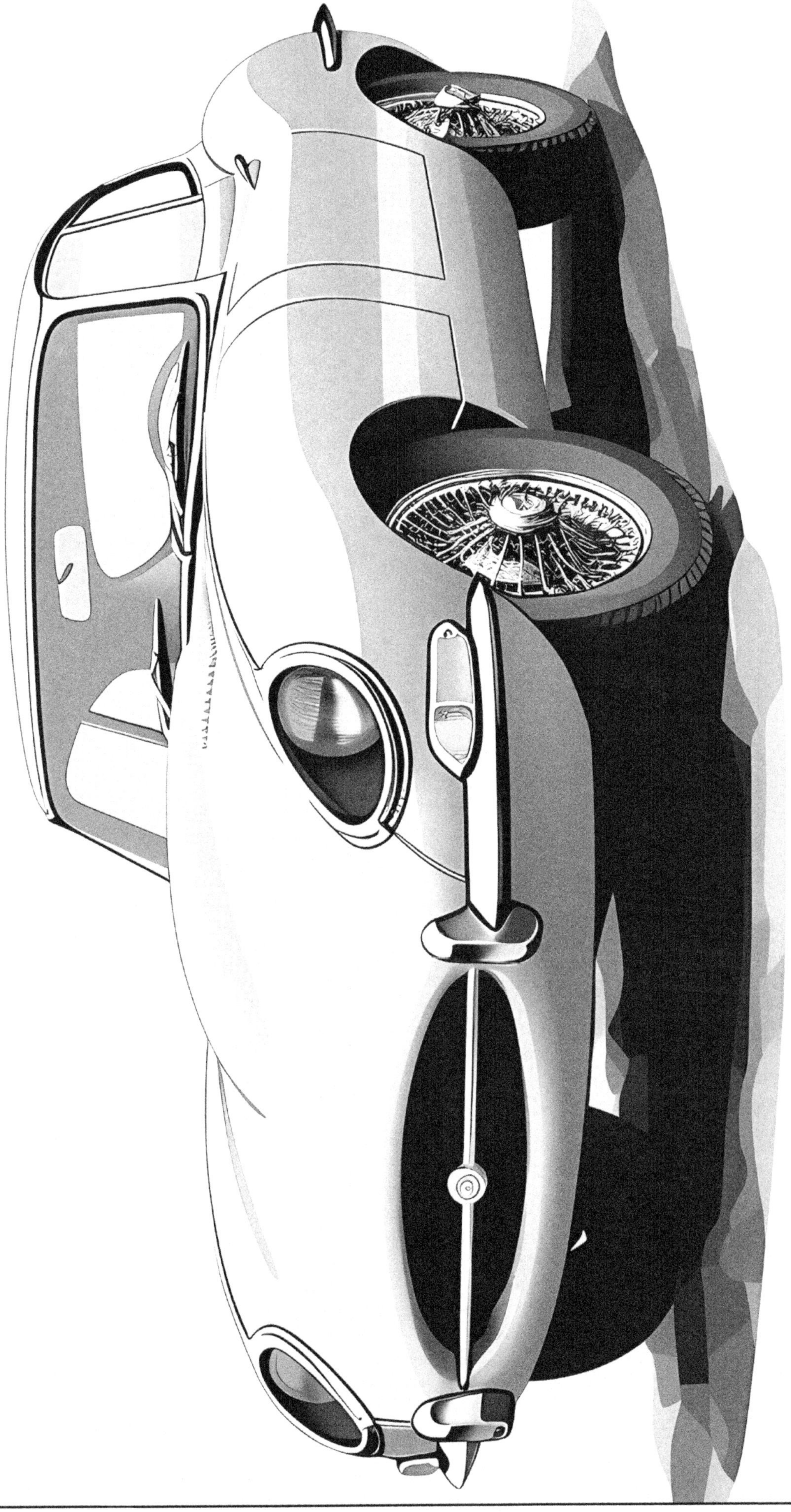

Printed in Dunstable, United Kingdom

65090712R00114